PRESENTED TO:

_____

FROM:

_____

DATE:

_____

Stories We Heard About Love

ON OUR TRIP ACROSS AMERICA

Bruce Bickel & Stan Jantz

Copyright © 2001 by Bruce Bickel and Stan Jantz
Published by J. Countryman, a division of Thomas Nelson, Inc.,
Nashville, Tennessee 37214.

Project editor—Terri Gibbs

Designed by Uttley/Douponce DesignWorks, Sisters, Oregon

ISBN: 08499-5735-4

Printed and bound in China

CONTENTS

Behind every Life
is a Story.

Introduction

We're two ordinary guys, but we had an extraordinary adventure. We spent the summer driving across the country. Now, that event isn't extraordinary in itself. In fact, many people have performed the feat. But most folks drive across country in an attempt to complete the task as quickly as possible. The memories of those trips are long hours on the inter-state, fast food wrappers scattered on the car floor, and no personal contact with anyone except the cashiers at the old-fashioned gas stations (the ones that have pumps and don't accept credit cards) and the occasional tollbooth operator. (People who are in a real hurry, or particularly anti-social, save time and avoid contact with even the tollbooth operator by keeping lots of coins in the car and using the "exact change" lane.)

Our trip was different. It extended over three and one-half months, so speed was obviously not an issue. We drove over 10,000 miles (which proves we didn't take the short route). But the *duration* and *distance* are not what made our trip extraordinary. The most intriguing aspects of our trip were the *people* we met and the *stories* they shared with us about their lives.

The purpose of our trip was to interview people. We were doing the research for a book (*Bruce & Stan Search for the Meaning of Life*), so we spoke with everyone, everywhere (even tollbooth operators and gas station cashiers). We had meaningful conversations with over 1,000 people. (That figure *doesn't* include the people we passed on the street or sat next to on the subway or stood next to in the elevator, with whom we exchanged limited pleasantries. Actually, we didn't even exchange pleasantries with the people in the elevators. We didn't want to break the unwritten rule of elevator etiquette, which prohibits talking or making eye contact.)

We expected to learn a lot about the meaning of life by talking to people (and we did). We learned so much, it could fill a book (and it has). But the unexpected pleasure was hearing the personal stories of the people we met. We heard fascinating stories about people. Some of the stories involved tragic events; some were encouraging. All of them were life changing—for the people who actually lived the stories and for us as we heard them.

Our lives will not be the same because of the people we met and the stories we heard. If for no other reason, we have a greater appreciation for people because we learned this very important lesson: *Behind every life is a story!*

What makes these stories so amazing is that they involve regular people. We didn't talk to any celebrities. Just plain folk. People like us . . . and you. (This assumes that you aren't chauffeured around in a limo and that you don't live in a mansion. If you're like us, you're more concerned about paying the mortgage than avoiding the paparazzi. If fact, we are only interested in "paparazzi" if it's a new flavor of Ben & Jerry's ice cream.)

In this book we've included ten of our favorite stories we heard while "on the road." They all have a common theme of love. But don't let that theme mislead you. People often restrict the definition of love to romance. Well, romance is an aspect of love, and we have a story or two that will emphasize that. But love can involve emotions that go much deeper than candlelight, cuddling, and Cupid. In this book we've included stories that illustrate a love defined by loyalty, devotion, self-sacrifice, humility, perseverance, and reconciliation.

We hope you'll be inspired by these stories. We were.

Maybe they'll motivate you to reflect on your personal stories and the lessons you can learn from your own life. Perhaps they'll make you more interested in the life stories of your friends and your neighbors. Maybe they'll encourage you to be more interested in the people you don't know as well. Remember: *Behind every life is a story!*

Bruce & Stan

OUR TRIP ACROSS AMERICA

BRUCE & STAN

Love Is Hospitable

We spent a lot of time in cities as we traveled across America. Cities like Boston, New York, Chicago, and San Francisco, where the sidewalks are packed with people and the pace is frantic. Cities are exciting, and they have lots of character, but they can be lonely places as well. Even though people constantly (and quite literally) rub shoulders with each other as they go about their business, they don't really notice one another. When you walk down Fifth Avenue in New York or Michigan Avenue in Chicago, all you see is a sea of faces. These aren't individual people. They're a mass of humanity.

We were ready for a break from the urgency of the urban, so we did what anyone who wants to get back to simpler times and a slower pace would do. We visited grandma and grandpa. They weren't our real grandparents, but they sure could have been.

From the time we walked into the home and the lives of Louise and Kirk Neely, otherwise known as Memaw and Bebop, we felt as if we'd known them forever. More significant, they made us feel like we were the most important people in the world that evening. They gave us the same kind of hospitality and love they've given to thousands of friends, hundreds of family members, and more than a few strangers over the years. They fed us, sat with us in the parlor, listened to our stories, and then told us theirs.

Memaw and Bebop live in a large, rambling Tudor-style house at the end of a wooded lane in the deep South. It's the kind of place you dream about visiting for Thanksgiving dinner or Sunday supper or anytime you need to get away from the rush and rumble of life. In Memaw and Bebop's house, there's no rush, and no one is a stranger, which is quite an accomplishment, considering the number of people who visit them.

Memaw and Bebop have eight children—four boys and four

Don't forget to show hospitality to strangers, for some who have done this have entertained angels without realizing it.

HEBREWS 13:2

girls—and sixty-eight grandchildren. Yet that only begins to tell the story of the number and variety of people who have been drawn under the warm canopy of their hospitality over the last fifty years.

For I was hungry,
and you fed me. I was thirsty,
and you gave me a drink.
I was a stranger, and you
invited me into your home.

MATTHEW 25:35

It all starts with family, of course. Kirk Neely owns a lumberyard, and Louise has always wanted a big family. When they designed and built the family home on Four Mile Branch Road thirty years ago, they made sure each of their children had a bedroom. The house still has eight bedrooms so their sons and daughters and their spouses always have a place to stay anytime they return "home." Even though the grandchildren don't have their own bedrooms, they come all the time, especially when it's time to decorate the house.

At the beginning of every major holiday season—Thanksgiving, Christmas, Easter, even the Fourth of July—Memaw decorates her home in a way that would put Martha Stewart to shame. It's legendary. And it's the grandchildren who help.

"She decorates this entire house sitting in that chair," Bebop remarked, pointing to Memaw, who sits in the same chair whenever company comes (which is just about all the time). "We'll have as many as fourteen grandchildren in here for a weekend when Memaw decorates the house. She'll say to one of the kids, 'Go upstairs and look in the hall closet. On the second shelf, halfway down, you'll find a box marked such-and-such. Bring me that box.' And she'll get the box, pull out a picture or some decoration, and say, 'This goes near the back door on that piece of furniture.'"

And so it goes. Box by box, grandchild by grandchild, the house gets decorated for a special season or event. And yet somehow you know it's not the decorations that matter as much as the relationships Kirk and Louise are building with their family, their friends, and strangers like us. We were with them a week before July Fourth, and sure enough, there was Burke, a grandson in his late teens who loves to spend time with Memaw and Bebop. We asked him what was so special about being with his grandparents.

"Memaw is so welcoming and so loving," said Burke. "Bebop is humble and generous. You know he'd do anything for you. He cares."

Without knowing it, Burke has defined the essence of hospitality. It's what Memaw and Bebop are all about. Their demonstrable

The Tudor-style house where we met Meman & Bebop.

love for friends and strangers alike started early in their marriage—and it hasn't stopped. They began by inviting families from church to their home on Sunday nights (Louise worked in the nursery and Kirk taught adult Sunday school), and it grew from there. Now families and Sunday school classes from dozens of churches all over town come over for special dinners, especially at Christmas when the house is decorated with the staggering array of lights, ornaments, and accessories Louise has collected over the years.

Through the years, children have always been the focal point of any Neely gathering. There's never been a time when Memaw and Bebop haven't been raising, influencing, and loving children. "Louise has always had a way to talking to children so they respected her," said Kirk. "And she never raises her voice."

Kirk supported his wife in everything she did,

*Bebop & Memaw—
the perfect hosts.*

*The world is full of places to go,
but your home should be the place where
people want to stay.*

and it showed in his philosophy of raising children. "It's the simplest thing in the world," he said. "All you have to do is make the children understand that they have to obey their mother."

"Prayer has been a key ingredient in our family," said Memaw, "especially when it comes to our children's relationship with the Lord. We can pray for children, pray with children, but we should never try to over-persuade them. Let them know that Jesus loves them, and when it comes time for them to pray to receive Jesus, it needs to come from their hearts."

Maybe that's why so many people claim Louise and Kirk as their Memaw and Bebop. It's not just their love you feel, but the love of God as well.

"Is that the key to showing true hospitality?" we asked Memaw.

The Neely dinner table is always set for friends.

"Anyone can do what we're doing," she responded. "But you have to make some decisions first. The first thing you need to do is to dedicate your home to the Lord. Tell Him you want it used if He so chooses. Ask Him to help you show His love and His joy to everybody who comes into your home. Let the Lord do it. He has to do it. I didn't set out to do what I'm doing. I've been amazed at the way the Lord has used us and our home and the people who've been here. It's just unreal."

Perhaps a small plaque on a wall in the Neely home best sums up their gift of hospitality:

> *There are no strangers here*
> *Just friends we haven't met*

No one has kept track, but close friends estimate that the Neelys have entertained tens of thousands of people—friends and strangers alike—in their home over the years, and Memaw and Bebop have loved every one of them. Truly their hospitality is a gift from God, and their love is a blessing to all they meet.

OUR TRIP ACROSS AMERICA
BRUCE & STAN

Love Releases

It was graduation week when we visited the campus at Harvard University. The quad, known as Harvard Yard (pronounced "Hahvad Yahd") was filled with parents preparing for the emotional dichotomy known as "commencement." You could actually read the mixed emotions etched into their faces:

- *sadness*—that this event marked their child's passage of growth into adulthood;

- *pride*—that their child had accomplished the worthy and admirable goal of graduating from one of America's loftiest academic institutions; and

- *relief*—that the tuition payments, also lofty, were coming to an end.

Things can be replaced. What can't be replaced are people and relationships.

ONYOUROWN.COM

But the prevailing and pervasive emotion was love. It was evident in the conversations between the parents and their students. Frequently it was expressed by the student with words of gratitude for tuition payments made on his or her behalf. Other times, love was heard in the parents' words of admiration for their student's scholastic diligence (on the mistaken assumption that those bloodshot eyes were caused by long hours studying in the library).

Each of us has a daughter, and each had received her college diploma just a few weeks before. We knew what these parents and students at Harvard were going through.

What we already knew, and what they were soon to learn, is that love requires *releasing*—both by the parents and by the students.

It's easy to tell when the parents come to the realization that they must release their child. You can hear mothers sobbing and fathers sniffling during the commencement program. That's when they comprehend that they must release their child to "the real world." Their weeping is an acknowledgment that they must step back and let their child fly (or fall). It's part of life.

The process of releasing is even more excruciating

A view of one of Harvard's chapels.

As you get to know
God a little more each day,
your life will take on
more meaning and you will
feel more fulfilled.

ONYOUROWN.COM

for the students. But it doesn't happen during the graduation ceremony. It usually occurs about a month later, after they've moved out of the dorms and established a life on their own. It happens when they start to receive bills for rent and utilities addressed to them instead of their parents. For these students at Harvard, they would learn soon enough that love means releasing their parents from financial bondage.

As we walked past those ivy-covered buildings in Cambridge, Massachusetts, we could have sworn we heard the agonizing shrieks of our daughters in California as they learned the lesson . . . that love releases.

We entered every city and town on our trip without any fanfare. That wasn't difficult to do, because nobody knows who we are (or cares). If we are legends at all, it is in our own minds. (We like to refer to ourselves as "the most famous people you never heard of.") But occasionally, on a slow news day, a newspaper or radio reporter would be assigned to cover "our story"—two guys driving across the country in search of the meaning of life.

When we were in Spartanburg, South Carolina, we were interviewed by Benny Smith, a reporter for the Herald-Journal. Benny was a friendly young man. He had too much experience to be considered a "cub" reporter, but he hadn't been on the beat long enough to be jaded. He

Live your life so that when you
die, people will know that you
  —loved others clearly
—loved your family dearly
—loved God completely.

GOD IS IN THE SMALL STUFF
FOR YOUR FAMILY

hadn't yet lost his enthusiasm for life. We considered him to be bright, insightful, and perceptive. (This is an objective opinion that hasn't been influenced by the nice article he wrote about us.) Benny was professional as he interviewed us for interesting angles about the meaning of life. We gave him some of our best material, but the stories we told to Benny weren't nearly as interesting as the story he told us . . .

Benny lives in an upstairs apartment. Below him live Bob and Lib Wood. The Woods are seventy-something seniors who have called Spartanburg home for most of their lives. As they entered their retirement years, they sold the house they had lived in for forty years and moved into Benny's apartment complex—and into his life.

Many people in our American culture never get to know their neighbors. For most people, it's a game of intentional avoidance. Maybe you're one of them. Perhaps

Relatives are the part of your family you're stuck with. Close friends are the part of your family you choose.

---

you drive home from work and shut the garage door behind you, sealing yourself inside and the rest of society outside. Or, maybe you pass your neighbor in the apartment hallway, but you avoid any eye contact by pretending that you have a stiff neck and twisting your head to the opposite side as you walk by. (This technique usually works fine—because you neighbor doesn't want to see you either—unless he or she is a chiropractor, and then you're likely to be confronted with a business card and discount coupon for the fifteen spinal adjustments to cure your neck spasm.)

But Benny and the Woods aren't alienated neighbors.

They're more like close family. In fact, when Benny's grandmother died, the Woods filled the role of surrogate grandparents for him. Benny would greet them each day as he walked by their apartment on his way to work. They were usually in their living room reading the newspaper. Bob would often give Benny some last-minute fashion tips to help coordinate a shirt and tie. Bob and Lib even added to Benny's wardrobe by giving him a Christmas tie.

The friendship between Benny and the Woods transcended their daily greetings. Benny could often be found spending time with Bob and Lib. Usually they just shared a good conversation, but occasionally he would help them by moving furniture or programming their VCR so the correct time would display instead of con- stantly flashing 12:00. (We could use Benny at our houses

Benny and his friends,
Bob & Lib.

for the same reason.) Each visit seemed to strengthen their friendship.

The depth of their relation- ship was demonstrated at 1:00 A.M. one morning. The ring of his phone awakened Benny. It was Lib calling. She frantically explained that Bob was having trouble breathing and needed to be taken to the hospital. In a "quick-change" routine that would make Clark Kent jealous, Benny was out of his pajamas and into his jeans and shirt in an instant. He bounded downstairs, assisted Bob into the car, and drove the Woods to the hospital emergency room (setting a new land-speed record in the process).

At the emergency room, Bob was whisked into a treatment area, and Lib accompanied him. Benny sat in the waiting room and waited. (Please forgive our redundancy). And he continued to wait. After three hours, he approached the clerk and requested information and an update on Bob's condition. The clerk said that such information could only be given to a family member. Without intending to be deceitful, and based on the closeness of his relationship with the Woods, Benny replied: "But I am family."

Now you might think the clerk should have accepted Benny's statement at face value. But that was part of the problem. The clerk, who had seen Benny arrive with the Woods, was only looking at face values. You see, Benny's face is black and the Woods' faces are white. The clerk must have been thinking that this "family" was stretching the bounds of genetic credibility.

At that moment, Bob and Lib appeared and told Benny the good news that Bob's problem was not serious. The three of them did a "group hug" right there in the waiting room. This must have been a strange sight to the clerk and the other folks waiting there in the hospital: A young black man hugging an elderly white couple, with a mixture of laughter and tears, as they celebrated life and their affection for each other. But it shouldn't seem strange at all. Isn't that how we expect families to act with each other?

Thankfully, this is as close as Bruce & Stan got to Capital Hill.

Bruce tries to climb his way into the White House.

OUR TRIP ACROSS AMERICA

BRUCE & STAN

OUR TRIP ACROSS AMERICA

Love Never Gives Up

When Bjorn Johnson—or BJ as his family and friends call him—hits a golf ball, it's a thing of beauty. He's tall, slender, and at sixteen his Swedish heritage makes him look like a blond Tiger Woods. Not that BJ has aspirations to be the next PGA champion. He simply enjoys playing golf with his dad and his friends—or even by himself if there's no one around. When the Texas heat keeps everyone else in the clubhouse, BJ loves to "hit 'em straight and long" down the fairways.

It wasn't supposed to be this way, not according to the doctors and attendants who watched as BJ's mother, Jeanie, struggled to give birth to her son at twenty-four weeks—*three months* before he was due. If the medical professionals had prevailed sixteen years earlier, there would be no golf swing, no mornings spent walking the fairways. There would be no joy in the Johnson family— at least not the joy this young man has brought them and so many others. There would be no BJ.

The Johnson family—Ken, Jeanie, and their two boys, Erik and Bjorn—used to live in California, which is where we first met them. Ken's job moved them to Plano, Texas, a boomtown just north of Dallas. That's where we connected with the Johnsons, who were eager to talk about their living, breathing, golf club swinging miracle. We met for dinner at the Country Club. BJ would have joined us, but he was finishing a round of golf. With the beautiful backdrop of St. Augustine grass and majestic Texas Oak trees, Ken and Jeanie told us the story of BJ.

"Medically speaking, I had a nearly zero percent chance of conceiving," said Jeanie, a nurse who specializes in

Love never gives up,

never loses faith,

is always hopeful,

and endures through

every circumstance.

1 CORINTHIANS 13:7

BJ Johnson now at 16 years old.

oncology. "I had two and a half pages of complications. Erik's birth had been a miracle. He arrived full term and 100 percent healthy. Two years later Ken and I got pregnant with Bjorn, and for the first five months everything was fine."

Then the unthinkable happened. Twenty-four weeks into her pregnancy, Jeanie's water broke. She was hospitalized immediately, and four days later she became septic with a fever of 104. Still, she hadn't gone into labor, which concerned the doctors. "They wanted to induce labor with the intention of aborting my baby," Jeanie said. "I asked for a C-section, but they didn't want to do that because, in their words, the baby wasn't *viable.*"

One day before BJ was born, another resident came to Jeanie and said, "This hospital doesn't consider 24 weeks to be viable." In her weakened condition, Jeanie sat up in bed and focused on the resident with a look that only a laser could duplicate. "Then you send me and my son somewhere where they do!"

You only have to spend a few minutes with Jeanie to realize that she's feisty. Ken is practical, predictable, and steady, but Jeanie holds nothing back. Not now, not ever. When the doctors in that California hospital said her baby wasn't *viable,* they had no idea of the magnitude of passion and will they had just unleashed in this young mother.

The doctors were puzzled. Here was this extremely pre-mature baby who refused to die, and then there was his "pro-life" mother who refused to give up hope. A female resident came to Jeanie and told her that the doctors were going to have a conference. "What do you want us to do?" she asked.

"I want this baby," Jeanie replied.

"Then I will go to bat for you."

As it turned out, at the doctors' conference the resident was the only one in a roomful of men to advocate saving BJ. So it seemed that nearly everyone on the hospital staff was fighting for death. Who would stand up for BJ?

"They wanted to induce labor with the intension of saving my life, but that would also abort the baby," Jeanie said. "After eight hours and no contractions, they increased

the level of Pitocin
against my wishes,
and wanted to
sedate me with
Valium. I refused
because I wanted to be
fully alert. I told them, 'If this baby
dies, I want to be there.'"

BJ Johnson at
24 weeks old,
wearing his
father's ring.

But the baby didn't die. On
September 20, 1984, Jeanie deliv-
ered a boy. She had wanted another
son, and she asked the doctor what she had.

"It's a boy," the doctor gasped and then said in disbelief,
"and he's breathing!"

BJ fit into the doctor's hand. He was blue-green, "like a
frog," and weighed just one pound, seven ounces. He was
barely twelve inches long. The umbilical cord was still

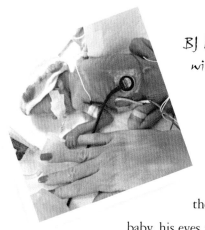

BJ holding hands with his mother.

pulsating when they cut it, and when the anesthesiologist saw the baby, his eyes registered shock.

But BJ didn't take just one breath. He took a second breath, and then another. He may not have been kicking, but he was alive.

One of the most critical debates in our culture concerns the issue of abortion. There is so much rhetoric thrown around that it's hard to sort out the truth. But the truth is there, and it's straight from the Bible: *"You made all the delicate, inner parts of my body and knit me together in my mother's womb"* (Ps. 139:13).

Long before BJ was born, Ken and Jeanie knew that this precious life wasn't just a viable or non-viable piece of tissue. This was their child, knit together by God, part-by-part, molecule-by-molecule. From the moment he was conceived, everything that made Bjorn the person he would become was present and intact as God's miraculous gift of life. It was only a matter of time before his body caught up with the real BJ.

———————

Four days after BJ was born, he was still alive, the earliest surviving infant ever recorded in California at the time. But his medical complications were incredible. There was no logical reason why this tiny infant should continue to live.

As you get to know God a little more each day, your life will take on more meaning and you will feel more fulfilled.

ONYOUROWN.COM

This is where the story really gets good, because this is where love took over. The love of Ken and Jeanie for their helpless son. The love of countless numbers of friends and family praying for BJ with passion and purpose. The love of the hospital chaplain who prayed over BJ's incubator every single day. And the love of a doctor from South Africa by the name of Hezekiah, who spent an entire night praying for BJ as he placed one of his hands on the incubator and the other hand on the chart.

Most of all, it was the love of God for His precious child that mattered most. Is anything too small for God?

Is anything too hard? Never! Out of His love for BJ, God gave him life, and then He gave him much more—the will to live.

"All through his time in the hospital—130 days in all—I could sense Bjorn's incredible will to live," Jeanie recalled. "Even after we brought him home—and throughout all his life—BJ has faced incredible physical challenges. I've even asked myself, 'Did I do the right thing?' Then one day I realized that my decision to fight for BJ was only one part of the process. God showed me in His Word that He was the one who had cared for BJ in the hospital, and He would care for him every day after that."

I created you and have cared for you since before you were born. I will be your God throughout your lifetime—until your hair is white with age. I made you, and I will care for you. I will carry you along and save you (Is. 46:3–4).

Indeed, God cares for BJ, just like He cares for each

Babies can't help being cute, cuddly, and charming. It's what they do.

one of us. God cares for BJ when he plays golf, when he goes skiing with the church high school group, when he goes to school, and when his dad takes him on special business trips. And you get the feeling that when BJ is old and gray, he'll still be living life to its fullest, thanks to a family who loves him and a God who cares.

Jeanie never
gave up on BJ.

WE COME HERE TO REMEMBER
THOSE WHO WERE KILLED, THOSE WHO SURVIVED AND THOSE CHANGED FOR
MAY ALL WHO LEAVE HERE KNOW THE IMPACT OF VIOLENCE.
MAY THIS MEMORIAL OFFER COMFORT, STRENGTH, PEACE, HOPE AND SEREN

OUR TRIP ACROSS AMERICA
BRUCE & STAN

Love Remembers

emory can be a blessing or a curse. If you remember a person or an event so you can bring honor, that's a blessing. But if you remember for the sake of revenge, it's more like a curse.

Nowhere in America is the difference more clearly displayed than in Oklahoma City, home of the largest terrorist attack in U.S. history. The Oklahoma City bombing is one of those events seared in the memory of every person. Not only do you remember the event, you also remember where you where when it happened. That's why we decided to visit the Oklahoma City National Memorial built on the site of the bombing that took place on the morning of April 19, 1995, killing 168 men, women, and children.

Honestly, we didn't know what to expect. When it comes to "big time" monuments and memorials, you think of "big time" cities like Boston and Washington and their impressive monuments to national heroes and events. We had seen a bunch of these landmarks, such as the very moving Viet Nam Memorial in our nation's capital. So we didn't think we would be all that impressed by this new memorial in the Heartland.

We were wrong.

Nothing in our cross-country tour moved us like the memorial built in downtown Oklahoma City on the very site of the bombing. As you enter the memorial from either side, you pass through a gate that marks the time of the horrific event. The numbers on the east gate simply say "9:01" to commemorate the time one minute before the moment of destruction. The west gate says "9:03" to mark the time one minute after. It's as if the blast itself is

Whenever you encourage
others, you are showing that
you have care and concern
for them. Few things in life
are so easy to give and
have so much impact.

When we die, we leave everything
behind except the choice we made about
God during our life.

GOD IS IN THE SMALL STUFF
FOR YOUR FAMILY

---

suspended in time for one single purpose—to remember.

Everything about the Oklahoma City memorial is designed to encourage blessing rather than revenge. All you see are symbols designed to honor the victims, survivors, and all who were changed forever that day: the reflecting pond, the field of 168 empty chairs, the survivor tree, and the fence.

Ah yes, the fence. For years after the bombing the only memorial to the event was the chain-link fence that encircled the site. The fence became a gathering place for family, friends, and strangers to post their notes, photographs, Scripture verses, and stuffed animals. A portion of the fence remains to this day, and you can still read the notes and see the pictures. This is where the human faces come alive. This is where the names take on meaning. Most important of all, this is where you truly feel that love is most powerful when love remembers.

Looks can be deceiving. When you look at Roy Moses Pope and his wife, Zoe Anne, you would think that their life has been a fairy tale. Roy is a very handsome man (we don't mind saying that), and Zoe is strikingly beautiful. They have six children who adore them dearly, and they love each other with the kind of love you read about only in fairy tales.

In the case of Roy and Zoe Anne, the looks are real, but their lives are a different story. Oh, they have a beautiful life together, but it's a life born out of incredible pain, the kind of pain that will either break you or make you. In the Pope's case, it did both.

Before we even met Roy and Zoe Anne, we had heard

parts of their story. A lot of people in Central California, where they live, have heard their story. Hollywood needs to tell this story, but no one would believe it. There are so many twists and turns and coincidences that even to this day, Roy thinks of things he has never shared with Zoe Anne. And Zoe still remembers details she hasn't thought of since the day they happened. It's an ongoing story with new inspirations and new revelations popping up from time to time. What doesn't change is that this is a story about a love stronger than the tragedies and triumphs of life. Roy and Zoe Anne are living proof of that.

The call to preach and serve God full-time came to Roy Moses Pope when he was just a youngster in Kentucky. Later, while at Ohio Wesleyan University, he went to the Middle Eastern country of Lebanon for his junior year.

That's when he met Jeanne, who was also in Lebanon for her junior year from UCLA. Roy was your basic southern guy; Jeanne was a sophisticated world traveler. With his soft drawl, Roy took liberties with the English language; Jeanne

Roy and Jeanne begin their life together.

was fluent in French and Arabic (her parents had been missionaries in the Middle East). Yet it was love at first sight for both of them. They married in 1971, graduated from Fuller Seminary in 1975, and accepted their first pastorate in Kentucky. By the late 1970s, Roy and Jeanne had settled in Jeanne's hometown of Fresno, California, and by 1980 their third child was born. Life was good. God was good.

Mike Mendes was the all-American everything. He was a superior athlete at Fresno State University, where Zoe Anne was on the pep squad. They met in 1971, fell in love, and got married two years later. Mike had always wanted to fly. He was in the ROTC program at Fresno State, and then entered the United States Air Force's pilot training program in Lubbock and San Antonio, Texas.

During the six years Mike and Zoe

Mike is ready to take off in his Air Force jet.

Anne lived in the Lone Star State, they had two boys.

They had always wanted to return to Central California, where both their parents lived, so in 1981 Mike joined the Air National Guard in Fresno, a key West Coast defense base. He could fly F16s and still have time to work in his family's real estate business. Life was good. God was good.

The cancer that first showed itself in Jeanne's chest was like a pressure around her heart, as if a mysterious hand gripped it tightly. Jeanne had never been sick a day in her life, so it was inconceivable that she would have an illness, let alone cancer. That's why her diagnosis of advanced stage histiocytic lymphoma—an insidious kind of lymphoma that attacks and surrounds the body's vital organs—was such a shock. It was 1981, and Jeanne was 31 years old.

Jeanne was a beautiful and dignified person both inside and out. The chemotherapy was brutal both inside and out and took its toll on her physical condition and appearance. Because people all over the world prayed for her around the clock, her illness was very public. But when it came to the pain of her cancer, Jeanne chose to bear it alone. "She was a very private person," Roy recalls. "When the effects of the chemo would be at their worst, she would go into the bathroom and lock the door. Often I could hear her praying behind the closed door, crying out to God. One time I pressed my ear against the door, and I heard her utter this incredible prayer in between her anguished cries—

'Lord, if this is your will . . . if anyone can come to know you through this . . . then it's worth it.'

"I was so moved. Tears rolled down my face. My beautiful wife was *praising* God, wanting His *will* in the midst of

The only way to truly love your spouse is to love them with the selfless, "I want the best for you" kind of love that only God can produce in your life.

her terrible condition. All she wanted was to *glorify* God."

While Roy and Jeanne were experiencing their nightmare, Zoe Anne and Mike were living their dream. Mike wasn't just a Top Gun, he played one in the movies! In 1982 his squadron was filmed doing maneuvers over the California desert, and later the footage was used in the classic Tom Cruise movie. During the sequence, Mike's fighter jet broke away from the others in a symbolic "missing man" formation. It proved to be as prophetic as it was dramatic.

In the first part of 1982 Jeanne's cancer went into remission. For three months Roy and Jeanne believed a healing had occurred. Jeanne did some speaking in churches to encourage others, and Roy's life as a pastor resumed an

All praise to the God and Father of our Lord Jesus Christ. He is the source of every mercy and the God who comforts us. He comforts us in all our troubles so that we can comfort others. When others are troubled, we will be able to give them the same comfort that God has given us.

2 CORINTHIANS 1:3–4

almost normal routine. But the respite was just that—a temporary time of relief and rest. Another round of tests showed the cancer had metastasized. Jeanne only had months to live.

Roy and Jeanne were never as close and intimate as they were over the next few months. Friends and members of their church gave them a trip to Hawaii, but the real intimacy between them took place at home. This is where the real love story was written, man to wife, heart to heart. The doctors inserted a catheter that went right to Jeanne's heart. Because she wanted to be cared for at home, Roy took on the delicate task of inserting a fresh tube each day, carefully, lovingly, so Jeanne could live a little while longer.

For Jeanne, dying was a process of giving up things: the activities she enjoyed, the friends she cherished, and the appearance she guarded. But the hardest thing she had to give up was the ability to hold her own son, one-year-old Jordan. "Jeanne's death was like a constrictor squeezing the life out of her little by little," remembers Roy. "When that happens, the whole world takes on a different perspective."

While the cancer ravaged Jeanne's body, it didn't destroy her spirit. On November 1, 1982, she died with courage and dignity. Her husband, her mother, and her father were by her side, and they were the ones who saw the miracle of her passing from this life into the next. "It was the most amazing thing," Roy says with wonder. "As weak as she was, as much pain as she was in, she sat up in those final moments, her eyes as wide as I've ever seen them. But she wasn't looking at me. She saw something beyond me—beyond the room. She raised up her arms and opened her mouth, but no sound came out. Only this glorious expression of peace and joy. Then she collapsed on the bed and breathed her last."

———————

Three weeks after Jeanne's death, Mike went to Bible Study Fellowship and heard about a man with three kids who had lost his wife. "He came home that night very sad," Zoe Anne recalls. "He sat at the kitchen table and just stared out the window, at the stars. He couldn't help thinking about that poor young pastor, and he prayed that God would take care of him."

On the morning of November 30, 1982, Captain Mike Mendes had to make an early flight to Vancouver Island in British Columbia, so Zoe Anne bundled up the boys and drove her husband to the Air National Guard base. They didn't really converse—it's like that in the morning before dawn, especially when it's cold and raining outside—but when they got to the Guard air field they couldn't stop hugging and kissing. As Mike walked away from the car, Zoe's eyes followed his every step. "I thought to myself, he's so handsome and I love him so much."

Mike called when he got to Comox Airfield on Vancouver Island. He was going on a night mission, but he was really excited about going to the Young Life camp at Malibu the next day. Mike had made a decision to follow Christ at Malibu some years earlier, and he wanted to return to the spot. Zoe Anne felt a special longing for Mike that night, and she prayed extra hard after telling the boys a Bible story. She fell asleep, but then a pounding at the door in the middle of the night—the kind you never want to hear—startled her awake. It was her parents. And with great sadness they gave her some sketchy details about an apparent accident involving Mike.

Earlier that evening Mike had taken off in the dark and rain and was instructed by the air traffic controller to climb to 6500 feet and level off. But the controller evidently didn't realize that Prince Edward Albert Mountain was in Mike's flight path, and it measured exactly 6500 feet. Without warning Mike's jet clipped the top of the glacier peak, sheering off the bottom of his plane, killing Mike instantly. The collision caused an avalanche, burying the plane as it crashed on the other side.

All of this information was assembled much later, of

course. For the first few days all Zoe Anne knew was that there had been an accident. Officially, her husband was missing. Zoe prepared to fly to Canada, not to identify a body, but to see her husband again. "I dressed up and put on my makeup as if I *was* going to see Mike. I was going to see Mike!" But it wasn't to be. Before she could leave, Zoe Anne was told that a rescue team had confirmed Mike's death.

"It was like someone had taken a knife and plunged it into my heart," Zoe Anne says sadly. "I didn't know there was pain like this in the world.

The Air Force performs the "missing man" maneuver at Mike's memorial service.

I fell back on the bed as if someone had killed me."

The pain of Mike's death rolled over her in waves. The military escorted Mike's body to Fresno in a flag-draped coffin and the memorial service was set. Finally, at the height of her pain, in the depths of her despair, Zoe Anne called out to the only one she knew could comfort her. "Jesus help me!" she cried. Remarkably, although she continued to grieve, the unbearable aspect of her burden was lifted immediately, and it's never returned. "That day I prayed the greatest prayer anyone can pray."

———

Christmas 1982 was the loneliest of times for Zoe Anne Mendes and Roy Moses Pope. Zoe spent time with her family, but it wasn't the same. Roy wanted to take his three children to Disneyland to get their minds off their grief for a while, so on New Years Eve he traveled with them to Anaheim. He even checked into the Disneyland Hotel, but he didn't have the strength to go to the Happiest Place on Earth. After spending New Years in the hotel room, he piled the kids in the car and drove back to Fresno the next day. "When we got to the Central Valley, we encountered the worst fog I have ever seen," Roy recalls. "It took me six hours to drive 150 miles. When I finally got home I was exhausted, and then the phone rang."

On the other end of the line was the manager of a local Christian radio station. He had been trying to reach Roy for three days so he could invite him to be a guest on a special program entitled, "How a Christian Handles the Death of a Spouse." The show was already in progress, but for some reason Roy felt compelled to go. When Roy arrived at the station he noticed an attractive blond woman sitting in the broadcast booth. He sat next to her, and they ended up sharing a microphone. Zoe Anne took notice of the handsome man, of course, but she certainly wasn't looking for companionship.

"I had convinced myself, if I couldn't be Mike's wife, then I would be his widow." Evidently God had another idea.

Zoe Anne and Roy today, a couple very much in love.

Zoe Anne felt an immediate spiritual attraction to Roy. "I had never felt such a comforting presence," she says. For his part, Roy felt a strong spiritual confirmation. "It's hard to explain, but that first night in the radio station the Lord showed me in an instant what her life, her character, and her spirit

After Jeanne died, Roy found a journal she had been keeping. He discovered that she had been praying for his future wife.

were all about. I knew then that I wanted to marry her."

Some people would be troubled by the fact that Roy and Zoe Anne got married on April 16, 1983—just a few months after the deaths of their spouses. But the testimony of their lives together since that day stands as a miracle of love and of God. Most of us see our lives as a series of circumstances and coincidences, but for Roy and Zoe Ann, there are no coincidences. Just the hand of God guiding them through tragedy and triumph—for their benefit and for His glory.

When you talk to Roy and Zoe Anne, the spirit of love

between them and the spirit of God that binds them are clear and vibrant. Even their names speak to the miracle of their lives and their love. Zoe Anne calls Roy by his middle name, Moses, because it means *deliverer.* Zoe is the Greek word for *life,* and that's exactly what she is to Roy. Jeanne and Mike may be gone, but they are not forgotten. They live through the deliverance and the life that is Roy and Zoe Anne Pope.

Love Creates Opportunity

We weren't the only ones who took a cross-country tour last summer. Another group made a similar adventure, but the logistics—and significance—of their trip far exceeded ours. We tried on several occasions to re-route our journey so we could link up with them, but it never worked. So we kept track of them via the Internet because they posted a travel diary.

But wait, we're getting ahead of ourselves. This story is as much about the preparation as it is about the actual journey. Even the *idea* itself would have been rejected at the outset by most people. But sometimes love sees possibilities when reason just sees impracticalities. And Pastor Carol Houston has lots of love, so just about everything she sees is possible!

Carol is the minister of Bethel Unspeakable Joy Christian Fellowship Church in the Watts area of south central Los Angeles. Her congregation is comprised of African Americans who live and work in this inner city area. Many of the children in the church have never been outside of their neighborhood community. This area faces the unique challenges of many inner-city communities. But they also have something working in their favor that not even the most affluent communities in Southern California can claim—they have Pastor Carol.

Carol wouldn't approve of our heaping accolades on her. She's much too humble for that. She would want any tribute or praise directed to God. With Pastor Carol, everything revolves around God and the realization of His love. That's the motivation for the love she shows to others. So, we won't sing her praises too loudly (because we're sure she'll be reading a copy of this book). We'll just say that she's an amazing woman and leave it at that.

Pastor Carol has a heart for breaking down some of the cultural and ethnic barriers that seem to polarize our society. She was instrumental in establishing a program in her church that

Some of the children from Pastor Carol's church.

brings college students (who are typically white and relatively affluent) to live in the homes of church members during Spring Break.

While the news media focuses on the wild college scene at places like Fort Lauderdale and Palm Springs, Pastor Carol counsels college students about life in the inner city. The week ends with a better understanding of

Your biological family
is for a lifetime; your church
family is for eternity.

GOD IS IN THE SMALL STUFF
FOR YOUR FAMILY

ethnic diversities from both perspectives. Long-lasting friendships are forged between the college students and the members of the church. This program (called "Spring Break in the City") is the first opportunity for some of the college students to develop meaningful relationships with people from the Watts neighborhood.

Funny thing about love: It keeps your brain churning. When you love others, you're always thinking about them. You want what's best for them. That's how it is with Pastor Carol and the children of her church. Spring Break in the City doesn't give the children enough exposure to the world outside of Watts, so she's always thinking of other ways to expand the horizons of their lives.

Pastor Carol's brain was churning in July of 1999 while she was traveling on the East Coast. During a flight from Richmond, Virginia to Atlanta, Georgia, God gave her a vision. This wasn't just a little mental picture (remember, this is Pastor Carol we're talking about), it was more like an IMAX giant screen presentation with surround sound. God gave her the vision of taking the children of her church on a cross-country tour of the United States.

By the time her flight was over, Carol had already completed a budget for the trip. She figured that the cost per child would be $2,000. She determined to challenge each child to raise $1,000, and church would provide the matching $1,000.

Most people would see two big problems with this scenario. First, the families in Carol's church didn't have

$1,000 per kid just lying around for this purpose. Second, there was no money in the church budget to cover the matching cost for each child. But she looked at this adventure through the eyes of love—she saw right through the problems and knew that if God gave her the vision, He would provide the solution.

Imagine the skepticism of the parents in the church when Carol shared her vision. Many of the families had several children. (Even with the children jumping up and down with

Pastor Carol wanted the children to see Amercia.

excitement, it wasn't difficult to multiply the number of kids by $1,000 for each family and $1,000 for the church.) But Carol's love for the children wasn't going to let money stand in the way. She told them they would need to work for the money and not expect it to come easily.

To help the entire congregation share in her vision, Pastor Carol arranged for a touring bus company to send a bus by the church one Sunday morning. This was no dilapidated, run-down, rattletrap bus. It was a state-of-the-art, high

No ordinary church bus ... this is a touring coach.

Pity the poor children who receive a large inheritance instead of a rich heritage.

comfort, technologically advanced (meaning equipped with monitors and VCR) touring coach. (See, we told you. When Pastor Carol gets a vision, it's in full Technicolor!.)

The kids climbed aboard that Sunday morning to see what it was like. One of the youngest girls said, "This is my seat. This is where I'll be sitting when we tour America!" That little girl had no doubt God would provide her $2,000, and neither did Pastor Carol.

Carol was right. The money didn't come easily. It became a church-wide project. The children did odd jobs and fundraisers. And parents and friends of the church pitched in. One by one the children began to reach the $1,000 mark, but none of them stopped working when they reached their goal. They kept raising more money for the other children who didn't have enough.

On Monday, July 3rd, almost exactly one-year from the date that Pastor Carol had shared the vision, Youth Tour 2000 was ready to roll. Twenty-six wide-eyed, youngsters, ages nine to fifteen showed up at the church at 4:30 A.M. (The parents also showed up, but they weren't so wide-eyed or exuberant.) The prayer meeting began at 4:45 A.M. As you would expect, there were prayers for traveling mercies, but the common theme of many prayers was thankfulness to God for His faithfulness in providing the financial need of every child.

Summer Youth Tour 2000 traveled through twenty-nine states in twenty-four days. They traveled the southern route spending nights in Tucson, San Antonio, Houston and Mobile. Then they proceeded up the east coast with stops in Atlanta, Durham, Norfolk, Washington D.C, Philadelphia, and New York City. Their route home covered the northern states

This children saw many amazing sites.

with stops in Toledo, Chicago, Sioux Falls, Mount Rushmore, Yellowstone, Salt Lake City, and Las Vegas.

Each day was packed with new sights and adventures. Carol had the children take turns writing a travel diary, while others conducted devotions on the bus. We've read the travel diaries, and it seems they covered all of the basic of any cross-country tour: lots of rest stops (including one in Louisiana with a crocodile), major universities, small towns and big cities, national monuments, and various churches along the way. We're assuming the continental breakfasts at the motels and swimming were highlights for the children since those activities were mentioned prominently in the travel diaries.

We thought you might enjoy reading this entry from Wednesday, July 26th (the day before the trip ended):

Today was an exciting day! For starters, we got a chance to sleep in. Pastor Carol informed us last night that we could sleep late since our time on the bus today would be about 17 hours.

In less than two days, we'll be home. Currently we are traveling from Salt Lake City, Utah to Las Vegas, Nevada. Some of us are hoping that when we arrive in Las Vegas we will be able to go to Circus Circus to play video games and swim at the hotel, but we are patiently waiting for Pastor Carol's decision.

The bus ride from Provo to Las Vegas was fun. Pastor Carol allowed us to share with our peers our personal thoughts in regards to each person's behavior on the tour. This was fun because it allowed us to see ourselves in the eyes of the others. Pastor Carol did explain that this was not a time to get even or to be mean, but we were encouraged to give honest and constructive criticism. The boys got rated from 1 to 10 and the girls from 1 to 16. The boy who ranked number 10 and the girl who ranked number 16 had the best behavior. Among the girls, I was number 10. We wanted to rate our chaperones, but Pastor Carol told us that each of them was excellent.

When we arrived in Las Vegas, Pastor Carol decided that swimming was going to be the activity for the evening. I really wanted to go to Circus Circus, but we went along with her decision because it was hot. 104 degrees to be exact!

Tomorrow evening the tour will officially be over and I will be home with my friends sharing my experiences. I love you all!

You can't read the travel diaries without realizing that the lives of these children have been changed forever by this once-in-a-lifetime experience. It's amazing what love can do when it sees the possibilities instead of the impracticalities.

Enjoying the trip of a lifetime.

OUR TRIP ACROSS AMERICA

BRUCE & STAN

Love Commits

When a couple loves each other, it's natural for them to want to be married. Love is all about commitment, and the wedding ceremony is a celebration of a couple's commitment to each other.

Many couples choose the city of Las Vegas for their commitment ceremony. We saw quite a few wedding parties when we spent a few days there. It's easy to spot a bride and groom in any crowd of people in Las Vegas. (You can't count on them wearing a wedding dress and a tuxedo—sometimes they're dressed in Bermuda shorts and tank tops.) Here's the telltale sign that gives their identity away: They're the ones with wedding cake crumbs on the floor around their slot machines.

We were intrigued by the emphasis on weddings in this city. The chapels are lined up, side by side, on the old "strip." To our way of thinking, Las Vegas doesn't seem to be a great place for a wedding. Maybe we're just old fashioned (although we prefer the term "traditionalists"). We each got married in a *church.* At our respective weddings, there wasn't an Elvis impersonator anywhere in sight. (And there wasn't a topless bar on one side of the church and an adult video store on the other.)

Las Vegas is the city of neon lights.

We were glad to see that most couples avoided the cheesy chapels on the strip. Instead, they choose one of the

Before marriage, you should concentrate on finding the right person. After marriage, you should concentrate on being the right person.

GOD IS IN THE SMALL STUFF
FOR YOUR FAMILY

other two primary wedding options for their nuptials:

- *Extravagant.* These are the weddings held at the luxury hotels on the nicer side of town.
- *Thematic.* You can't think of a theme that they can't provide. Camelot, luau and Harley Davidson are three of the most popular.

Love is all about commitment.

Although Las Vegas prides itself on offering unique wedding ceremonies, there is something they all have in common: A big price tag.

The traditional wedding vows include a promise to love each other whether "richer or poorer." That's a beautiful sentiment and an admirable commitment. But if you have your wedding in Las Vegas, the cost can take you from richer to poorer in the duration of the ceremony.

OUR TRIP ACROSS AMERICA

BRUCE & STAN

Love Teaches

One of the best selling books of the last few years is a little jewel called *Tuesdays with Morrie.* No doubt you've heard of the book. Perhaps you've read it or seen the television movie based on the book. Written by Mitch Albom, an award-winning sports writer for the *Detroit Free Press, Tuesdays with Morrie* is a journal of sorts describing the relationship between Mitch and Morrie Schwartz, one of his former professors at Brandeis University.

We drove past Brandeis, which is just outside Boston, at the beginning of our cross-country tour. Since both of us had read *Tuesdays with Morrie,* we thought about Mitch and Morrie because the book concerns one of our favorite subjects: mentoring. We had no thoughts of visiting

Morrie, mainly because he's dead (oops, did we spoil the ending of the book for you?). And we had no plans to visit Detroit, which ruled out a Tuesday (or any day for that matter) with Mitch.

Still, we thought about Mitch and Morrie and mentoring as we left Boston and headed south. We thought about how valuable a book like *Tuesdays with Morrie* is to people of all ages. If you're younger, you can identify with Mitch, a successful yet dissatisfied person who was drawn to Morrie when he learned that his old professor was dying of Lou Gehrig's disease. You're doing okay, but you know you have a lot to learn about life and relationships and how to find meaning in it all.

If you're older, you can identify with Morrie, not because you're going to die soon, but because you've learned a lot in your life. You have experience, you have wisdom, and you wish someone would listen to you, if only for a while.

A teacher
affects eternity;
he can never tell where
his influence stops.

—HENRY BROOKS ADAMS

That's the way it was with Morrie and Mitch. Morrie wanted to tell his story and teach someone what he knew about life. And Mitch was willing to meet regularly with his old professor, record his lessons, and care for his needs. At its essence, that's what mentoring is all about. Few of us ever take the time to initiate such a relationship, but all of us can learn from it.

Of course, since *Tuesdays with Morrie* has become such a national favorite, a lot of younger men and women like Mitch are looking for older mentors like Morrie (and it has nothing to do with writing a best seller, at least we

Tom Hunt—a real life mentor.

In the same way, encourage the young men to live wisely in all they do. And you yourself must be an example to them by doing good deeds of every kind. Let everything you do reflect the integrity and seriousness of your teaching.

TITUS 2:6-7

---

don't think it does). And there are plenty of older and wiser people around just dying (sometimes literally, sometimes not) to tell their stories. If such a mentor-student scenario appeals to you, that's great. Go for it. Find an older person to learn from, or identify a younger person to teach. Nothing but good will come out of such a relationship.

However, if you're looking for something a little more unusual, we think you'll find inspiration from a guy we met in Texas. His name is Tom Hunt, and he's one of the most dynamic and effective mentors we've ever met.

Along with being happily married, raising three daughters, and running a successful business, Tom has always had a passion to develop the lives of other men. When Promise Keepers came to Dallas a few years ago, he was there front-row center with several guys he knew who needed the message of accountability Coach McCartney and the other speakers were preaching. After the PK blitzkrieg left town, Tom mentored several of the men on a regular basis. He wanted to hold them accountable, and he wanted to be accountable to them.

When we first met Tom, we were warned that he had a vise-grip handshake. That's because Tom is an avid weightlifter. It's a hobby, but he takes his weightlifting seriously. We found out how seriously when we pulled into Tom's driveway. Both of his cars were parked outside because inside his garage was an array of weight machines that rivaled the local health club. Tom came out to greet us wearing a huge grin and huge muscles. We took turns shaking his hand (and quickly asked for an ice compress to reduce the swelling).

Lifting weights in Tom's garage

"The guys will be here soon," Tom said. We pictured a bunch of ex-marines and burly men with tattoos pulling up in trucks with over-sized tires and gun racks, ready to grunt and strain as they lifted Tom's weights. But that wasn't the case. Not with these weights. Not with Tom. The guys showed up all right, or should we say *boys.* One by one young teenage men with muscle shirts and weight-lifting gloves came to Tom's garage. They were high school sophomores, juniors, and seniors who came every Tuesday, Thursday, and Sunday nights to lift weights with Tom, their mentor.

"I enjoy working with men my own age," Tom said, "but I realized that I needed to reach guys at a younger age before they get stuck in their ways." So Tom decided to combine his passion for mentoring men with his passion for lifting weights. He put the word out that his garage would be open three nights a week for guys to come lift for an hour or so. Tom would instruct them, lift with them, and then afterwards they would "cool down" and talk. It wasn't long before the guys came and lifted and talked and it wasn't long before their discussions turned to serious matters, like life and relationships and God.

There's never any pressure. Tom isn't a Bible thumper, but he uses Bible study as a way to get these young guys to think about life's important lessons. We talked to a couple of dads who love it that their sons are lifting and learning with Tom. They agreed that Tom was a great role model, because he was showing them how to build spiritual as well as physical muscles.

Tuesdays with Morrie is a great book, and we encourage you to read it. But the example of Tuesdays, Thursdays, and Sundays with Tom is something that could be even more valuable to you. It's one thing to do what Morrie did, to teach about life from an earthly perspective. But it's even better to follow Tom's example of teaching others how to live with a heavenly perspective.

Bruce strikes a
sincere pose,
hoping
someone will
take his picture.

Stan can't
start his
day
without
Starbucks.

OUR TRIP ACROSS AMERICA
BRUCE & STAN

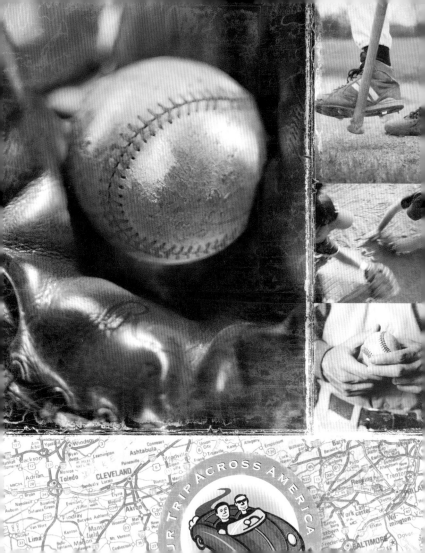

We're guys, so we like sports. We don't have any choice about the matter. It's embedded in our genetic code. While driving across the country, our daily routine included reading the sports section of *USA Today* in the morning and watching Sports Center on ESPN each night. (Most people select their lodging based on price or comfort. Our only criteria were a complimentary copy of *USA Today* and cable television.)

The world of sports is full of drama. There's the competition. The suspense. The thrill of victory. The agony of defeat. (We have to stop there. We're getting dangerously close to copyright infringement.) But when each game or match or tournament comes to an end, you know the outcome and the suspense is over. Just like other dramatic presentations, you know the ending when the curtain drops or the movie stops. You go home and file the event in your memory bank (for some future time when useless sports trivia will be necessary to impress your friends or win a bet).

But, occasionally, the drama of sports doesn't end when the game is over. Every once in a while there is some lingering, unresolved issue or conflict that survives long after the locker room has emptied and the fans' blood pressure has subsided. These stories seldom revolve around statistics. The interesting stories in sports that continue past the end of the game most always involve people and their relationship with each other. It's the dynamics of interpersonal relationships in sports that give us great stories of inspiration. Often what happens *on* the field is not as revealing as what happens *off* the field. In these situations, the real lessons are learned in the post-game wrap-up.

Even if you're not a baseball fan, you've probably heard about an incident on the field that shocked the sporting world not long ago. But maybe

The drama of sports doesn't end when the game is over.

you didn't hear the same "post-game wrap-up" that we did. In this case, what happened off the field is even more surprising than what happened during the game.

It was late in the summer of 1996. The Baltimore Orioles were playing the Indians at Jacobs' Field in Cleveland. Roberto Alomar, the Oriole second baseman, was at bat. John Hirschbeck was umpiring behind home plate. On a called third strike, Alomar lost his cool. He exploded in a tirade against Hirschbeck. The episode climaxed with Alomar spitting in Hirschbeck's face.

There has been no other time in the history of sports that the word "spit" appeared in more headlines or was spoken by more newscasters. This happened when baseball was struggling with its public image, and Roberto's loogie only made things worse. Every sports analyst and social commentator cited this incident as further proof that ball players were over-paid, ill-mannered ingrates.

Hirschbeck maintained a relatively low profile after the incident, but not Alomar. He held a press conference. Usually press conferences in such situations are used to defuse a tense situation. Not this time. It blew up in everyone's face (but no spit was involved this time). Alomar accused Hirschbeck of being distracted and failing to concentrate on the game. He said that Hirschbeck was still distraught and grieving over the death of his son,

Be as

good-mannered to people

behind their backs as you are

in their presence.

GOD IS IN THE SMALL STUFF
FOR YOUR FAMILY

John, who had died in 1993 from a rare brain disease known as adrenoleukodystrophy (ALD). The public perceived Alomar's comments as a "cheap shot." Even after serving his five-game suspension, he was booed wherever he played. As far as the public was concerned, Alomar wasn't worth . . . well, . . . spit.

As you can imagine, there was bad blood the following season between Alomar and Hirschbeck. They avoided each other. When Hirschbeck was a second-base umpire in a game with Alomar, Hirschbeck stood on the shortstop side of second base to avoid standing near Alomar at

> *"If [spitting on me] is the worst thing Robbie ever does in his life, he'll lead a real good life."*
>
> — JOHN HIRSCHBECK

the second baseman's position. (We guess he didn't want to be within spitting distance of Alomar.) The friction and latent hostility continued far into the 1998 season.

Maybe it was for love of the game, or maybe it was for the love of mankind. Whatever the reason, Hirschbeck wanted to break the tension. By this time, Alomar was playing for the Cleveland Indians. Hirschbeck's friend, Jack Efta, was in charge of the umpire's room at Jacob's Field, so Hirschbeck asked Efta about Alomar. Efta said, "Roberto is one of the two nicest people I've met. And you're the other one." That comment was enough to

"Maybe God put us in this world to help somebody beat this disease."

—ROBERTO ALOMAR

prompt Hirschbeck to contact Alomar. They went to dinner, talked things out, and made peace with each other.

The story would be nice if it ended there. But that's not the complete wrap-up. It gets better.

Since their peace treaty, Hirschbeck and Alomar have become very close friends. The focal point of that friendship is Hirschbeck's other son, Michael, who also suffers from ALD. John Hirschbeck and his wife have started a foundation to find a cure for this degenerative genetic disease that causes inflammation in the brain and afflicts 1,000 people each year in the USA. Roberto Alomar is one of the foundation's largest contributors, and one of its biggest fundraisers. At one charity event he sold his jersey (along with that of his brother, Sandy, who was the catcher for the Indian's) for $6,600. He also purchased jerseys for the entire team to wear during one game that were later sold at a charity auction for ALD.

Michael Hirschbeck has been an honorary batboy for the Indians. Guess who his favorite player is.

Roberto Alomar is still booed in several cities where he plays. Those fans only remember the story of his spit. It's unfortunate they missed the post-game wrap-up. That's the best part of the story. Just ask Michael.

More Stories

We invite you to read some of the other stories
we heard in the course of our cross-country tour of America.
They have been collected in three additional books:

Stories We Heard About Joy
Stories We Heard About Hope
Stories We Heard About Courage

And here are some other books we've written,
some of which are quoted in this one:

God Is in the Small Stuff
God Is in the Small Stuff For Your Family
OnYourOwn.com
Bruce & Stan's Guide to God
Bruce & Stan Search for the Meaning of Life

We'd love to hear from you. You can reach us by email at
guide@bruceandstan.com or through our Web site:
www.bruceandstan.com.